Let's Explore Canada

by Elle Parkes

LERNER PUBLICATIONS ◆ MINNEAPOLIS

Note to Educators:

Throughout this book, you'll find critical thinking questions. These can be used to engage young readers in thinking critically about the topic and in using the text and photos to do so.

Lerner Publications Company
A division of Lerner Publishing Group, Inc.
241 First Avenue North
Minneapolis, MN 55401 USA

For reading levels and more information, look up this title at www.lernerbooks.com.

Library of Congress Cataloging-in-Publication Data

Names: Parkes, Elle, author.
Title: Let's explore Canada / by Elle Parkes.
Description: Minneapolis : Lerner Publications, 2017. | Series: Bumba books. Let's explore countries | Includes bibliographical references and index. | Audience: K to 3. | Audience: Ages 4 to 8.
Identifiers: LCCN 2016044354 (print) | LCCN 2016045914 (ebook) | ISBN 9781512433616 (lb : alk. paper) | ISBN 9781512455564 (pb : alk. paper) | ISBN 9781512450378 (eb pdf)
Subjects: LCSH: Canada—Juvenile literature.
Classification: LCC F1008.2 .P374 2017 (print) | LCC F1008.2 (ebook) | DDC 971—dc23

LC record available at https://lccn.loc.gov/2016044354

Manufactured in the United States of America
1—CG—7/15/17

LERNER e SOURCE

Expand learning beyond the printed book. Download free, complementary educational resources for this book from our website, www.lernerresource.com.

Table of
Contents

A Visit to Canada

Canada is a country.

It is in North America.

Canada is north of the United States.

Canada has tall mountains.

It has deep lakes.

There are many forests.

Moose live in Canada's forests.

Moose have big antlers.

Fir trees grow in the forests.

Birch trees do too.

Canadians use wood from these trees

to build sleds.

What else do you think Canadians use wood to build?

Canada has big cities.

Toronto is the biggest.

The CN Tower is in Toronto.

The CN Tower is very tall.

13

Many people like

to visit Canada.

People ski down

the mountains.

They fish in the lakes.

What other things do you think people do in Canada's lakes?

Poutine is a popular food.

It has fries.

It has gravy and cheese.

Hockey is a top sport.

Many people play hockey.

Others like to watch it.

Why do you think Canada is a good place to play hockey?

Canada is a

beautiful country.

There are many things

to see.

Would you like to visit

Canada?

Map of Canada

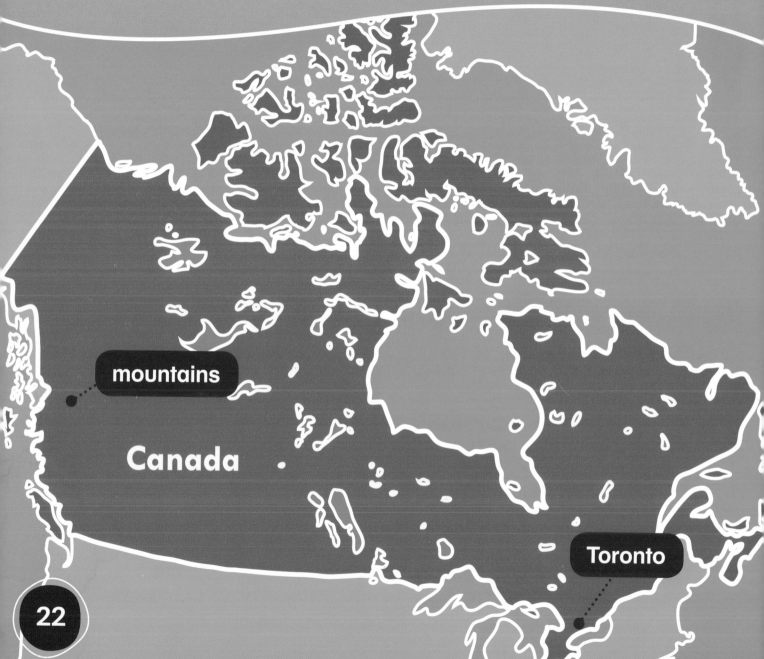

mountains

Canada

Toronto

Picture Glossary

hockey

a game where players skate on ice and hit a puck with a stick

moose

animals with big antlers that live in the forests of Canada

mountains

areas of land that rise very high above the land around it

poutine

a Canadian dish with French fries topped with cheese curds and gravy

Read More

Markovics, Adam. *Canada.* New York: Bearport, 2017.

Meister, Cari. *Do You Really Want to Meet a Moose?* Mankato, MN: Amicus, 2016.

Parkes, Elle. *Let's Explore Australia.* Minneapolis: Lerner Publications, 2018.

Index

Photo Credits